Engineering Wonders

SMART CARS

Kaitlyn Duling

Rourke Educational Media

rourkeeducationalmedia.com

Before, During, and After Reading Activities

Before Reading: Building Background Knowledge and Academic Vocabulary

"Before Reading" strategies activate prior knowledge and set a purpose for reading. Before reading a book, it is important to tap into what your child or students already know about the topic. This will help them develop their vocabulary and increase their reading comprehension.

Questions and activities to build background knowledge:

1. *Look at the cover of the book. What will this book be about?*
2. *What do you already know about the topic?*
3. *Let's study the Table of Contents. What will you learn about in the book's chapters?*
4. *What would you like to learn about this topic? Do you think you might learn about it from this book? Why or why not?*

Building Academic Vocabulary

Building academic vocabulary is critical to understanding subject content.
Assist your child or students to gain meaning of the following vocabulary words.

Content Area Vocabulary

Read the list. What do these words mean?

- accelerator
- aspects
- atmosphere
- autonomous
- components
- convert
- debut
- gasoline
- hybrid
- innovative
- nonrenewable
- parallel

During Reading: Writing Component

"During Reading" strategies help to make connections, monitor understanding, generate questions, and stay focused.

1. *While reading, write in your reading journal any questions you have or anything you do not understand.*
2. *After completing each chapter, write a summary of the chapter in your reading journal.*
3. *While reading, make connections with the text and write them in your reading journal.*
   a) Text to Self – What does this remind me of in my life? What were my feelings when I read this?
   b) Text to Text – What does this remind me of in another book I've read? How is this different from other books I've read?
   c) Text to World – What does this remind me of in the real world? Have I heard about this before? (News, current events, school, etc....)

After Reading: Comprehension and Extension Activity

"After Reading" strategies provide an opportunity to summarize, question, reflect, discuss, and respond to text. After reading the book, work on the following questions with your child or students to check their level of readi comprehension and content mastery.

1. What smart car innovations are being introduced in the auto industry? *(Summarize)*
2. In general, are cars becoming more or less safe? *(Infer)*
3. Why are engineers interested in building a fully autonomous vehicle? *(Asking Questions)*
4. How do you think you would feel riding in an autonomous car? *(Text to Self Connection)*

Extension Activity

Design your own smart vehicle! Will it have four wheels, fewer, or more? What kind of fuel or energy will it use get around? Will you incorporate steel, plastic, or other materials into its design?

TABLE OF CONTENTS

CAR IQ

When it comes to the world of automobiles, the variety is mindboggling. From sedans and sport utility vehicles (SUVs) to compact cars and pickup trucks, the options seem endless. Across the auto industry, engineers are buzzing about a type of car that has only grown more popular over the past 20 years: the smart car.

What is the difference between a traditional car and a smart car? The answer lies in advanced technology. Smart cars do more than just drive. Some use electricity to power their engines. Others drive all by themselves, without drivers! Can you believe it? These are truly the cars of the future.

Cars come in a variety of shapes, sizes, colors, and styles.

A traditional car gets a driver and passengers wherever they need to go. But smart cars do more. They are designed to solve common problems. One of these problems is environmental impact. Cars can pollute our world. How do they do this? A traditional car or truck has an engine that runs on **gasoline**.

During rush hour, the emissions pouring out of all those cars can create a smelly fog of pollution.

When the car burns gasoline, harmful substances are released into the air. These substances hurt our bodies, but they also help to heat up our planet's **atmosphere**. Cars contribute to global warming—the rising temperature of Earth's atmosphere, which changes weather patterns. With so many cars on the road, engineers have been working hard to find smart alternatives.

This doesn't mean that we all need to switch to bicycles! Many of the latest smart cars use electricity and other solutions to be much more environmentally friendly. They are also creating cars that help us combat overcrowding, car accidents, cost, and other problems.

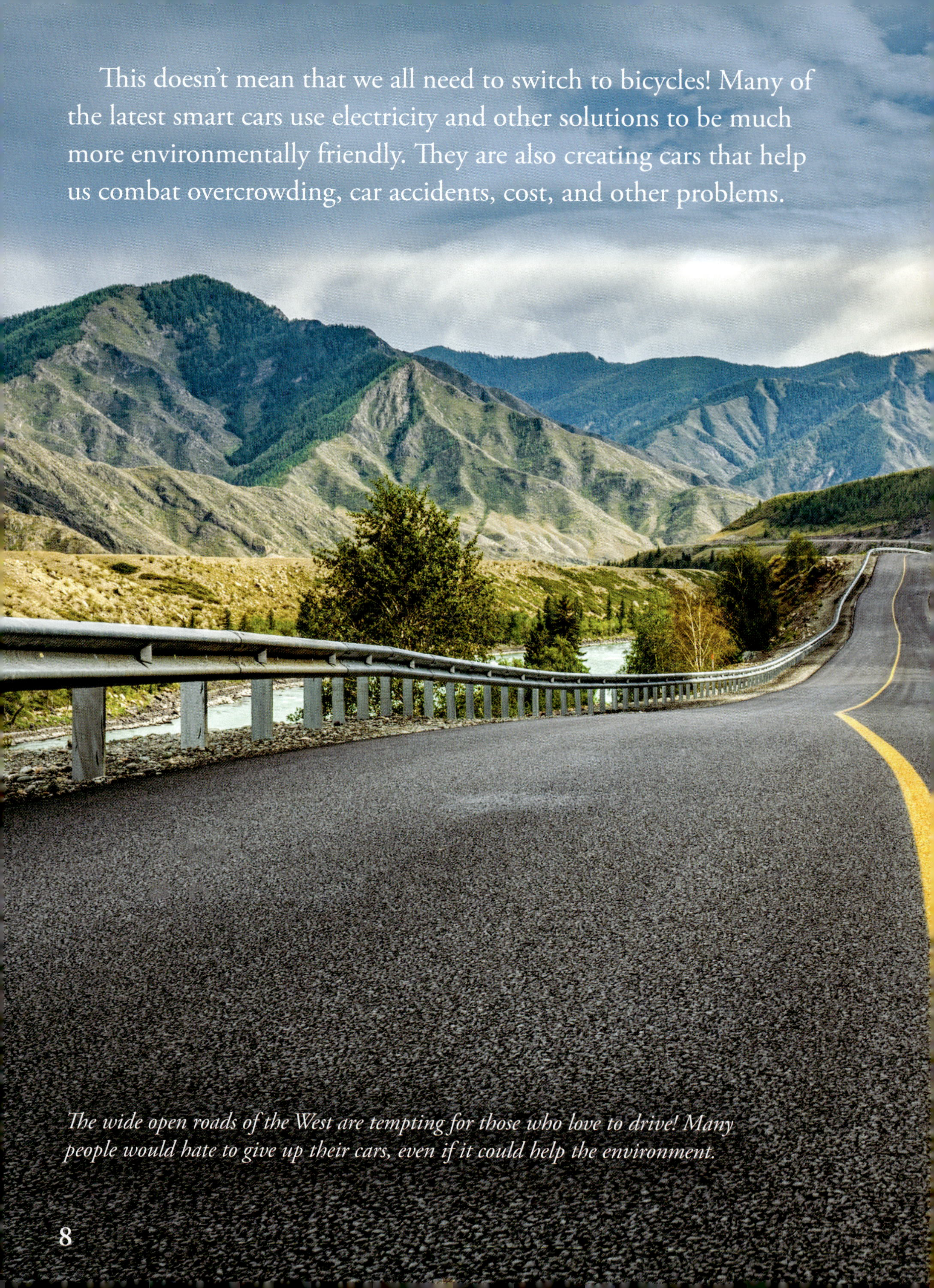

The wide open roads of the West are tempting for those who love to drive! Many people would hate to give up their cars, even if it could help the environment.

Need Directions? Ask Your Smart Car!

Since the 1990s, Global Positioning Systems (GPS) have become popular features in cars. They help drivers and passengers navigate while on the road. A smart car often has its own system or is able to communicate easily with phone technology.

DREAMING UP A SMART CAR

The world's first cars were created in the 1880s. That's less than 150 years ago! Cars haven't been around very long, but they've certainly made huge strides in their design and engineering. Most people credit Karl Benz, a German inventor, as the creator of the first car.

Karl Benz
1844–1929

Incredible Inventions
Karl Benz invented many of the parts we use in cars today, including the spark plug, ignition, carburetor, clutch, and gear shift, among others.

The very first cars, with their huge, thin wheels, looked a little like bicycles! This Motorwagen was built in 1885.

Now, a car that hits the automobile market has had an entire team of professionals working on all **aspects** of the vehicle. Automobile designers figure out what a car should look like, while automotive engineers focus on the technical aspects of how the car will run. An automotive engineer might work on a car's mechanics, performance, safety features, software, electronics, and so much more.

Think about the cars you see on the road. Some were produced by Ford or Chevrolet, others by Kia or BMW. The list of car manufacturers is long. Each of these companies produce new and updated car models each year!

As consumer tastes change, car companies continue to dream up new and improved designs. Over the past couple decades, those designs have become smarter and smarter.

Why are the cars getting smarter? Because humans are getting smarter about what we need and want our cars to do. When consumers demand cars that produce less pollution, drive safer, or fit into smaller spaces, the automobile designers and engineers respond by creating new cars. These fresh designs make their **debut** at annual auto shows that are scheduled around the world.

Luxury sports cars like the Mercedes-Benz EQ Silver Arrow are always a hit at auto shows. Their advanced technology and sleek designs are meant to surprise and stun the crowds.

Big auto shows in cities such as Detroit, New York City, Chicago, Tokyo, and Paris give people a glimpse into the future of automobiles. Smart cars are often on display at the shows, even if they won't be available to the public for a few years. These shows give attendees an inside look at the future of car design and engineering.

Auto shows offer practical solutions, too. At a car show in Frankfurt, Germany, a tiny, electric police car is on display.

SMART DESIGN AND ENGINEERING

So, what do the smart cars of the future look like? The designs that have emerged over the last few years are nothing short of incredible. Subcompact cars, **autonomous** cars, electric cars, and connected cars are four of the smart car categories that are pulling ahead of the pack.

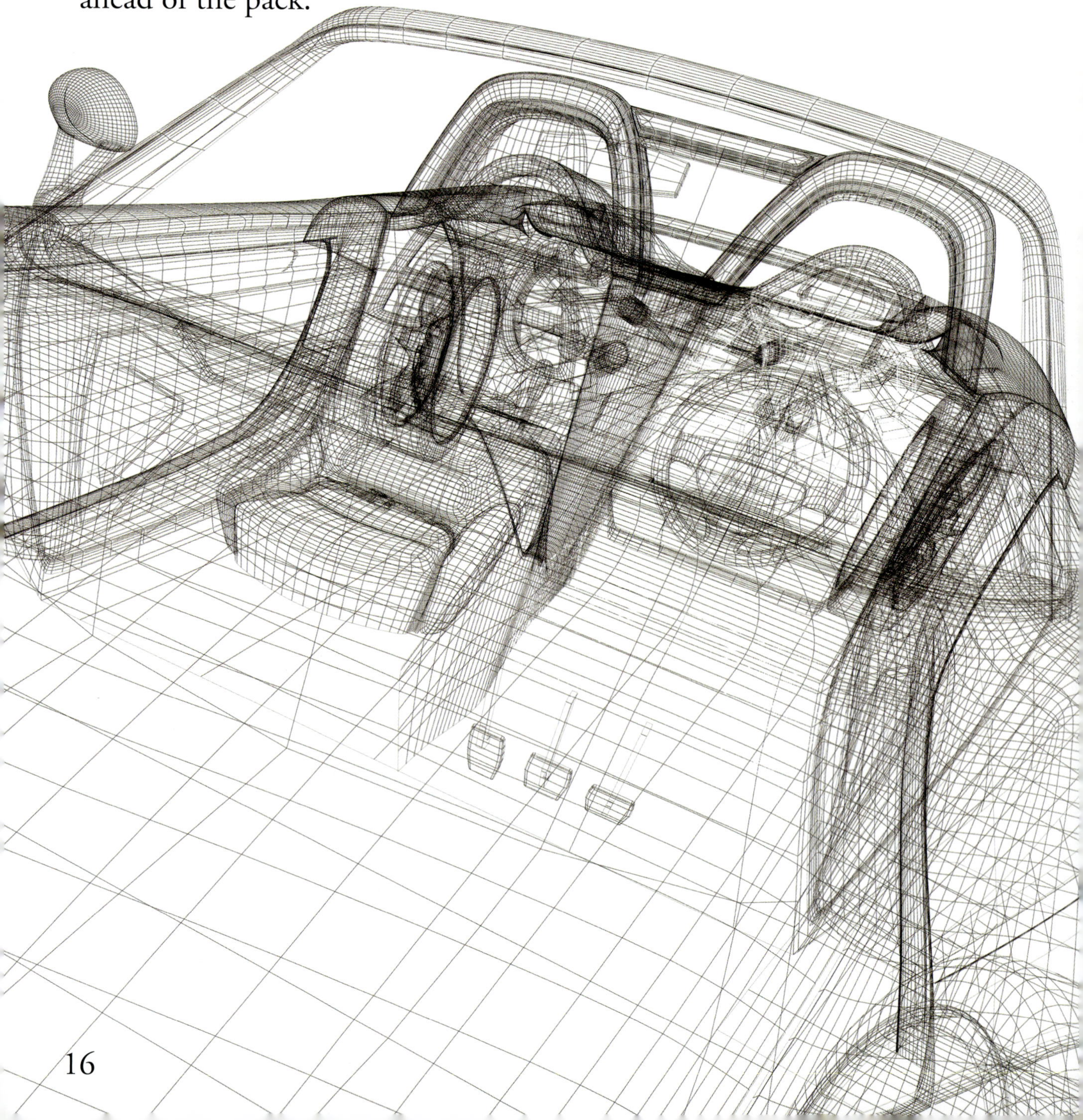

A subcompact car is similar to what you might imagine. It is a very, very small car! Small cars are called "compact cars," but subcompacts are even smaller. They are cute, efficient, and perfect for driving in the city.

They can change lanes quickly, make **parallel** parking a breeze, and use significantly less fuel than traditional cars. And they are often able to run on electric power!

This subcompact car is parked next to a traditional vehicle. It is almost half the size! This allows it to fit into smaller parking spaces and use less fuel.

Tiny Cars—Huge Demand

Some of the most popular subcompact cars include the Honda Fit, Ford Fiesta, and Toyota Yaris. They are usually much cheaper than traditional cars or sedans, often about 18 thousand dollars for a brand-new model.

The Honda Fit is a popular choice in the subcompact category due to its small size—and small price tag.

How do you use electricity to power a vehicle? Well, you plug it in! A micro-sized subcompact car might need to be plugged in for just a few hours before driving more than a hundred miles through the city. As it zips along the road, there aren't the usual gases and pollutants coughing out the back of the car. It is quiet, clean, and efficient.

Engineers actually developed the first electric cars back in the 1800s, but they quickly became overshadowed by gasoline-powered cars. Since the 1990s, environmental worries have pushed more and more car buyers to consider electric vehicles, especially in the subcompact category.

Hybrid cars such as the Toyota Prius have also become popular. These run on a combination of gasoline and electric power.

You can often tell a hybrid car by the logo on its body. You might also be able to pick out a hybrid by its lack of noise and emissions.

Henry Ford's Invention

Electric cars were hugely popular in the late 1800s and early 1900s, but they were priced out of the market with the introduction of Henry Ford's Model T. The Model T, powered by gasoline, was much cheaper and widely available.

As electric cars have gained popularity, another emerging technology has been on everyone's mind—autonomous vehicles, or self-driving cars. This phrase refers to cars that are able to navigate driving, turning, parking, and nearly every other task without the help of a human driver. You might think that autonomous vehicles are just a dream, but engineers have been working to turn them into a reality.

This show car, the smart EQ fortwo, dispenses with the steering wheel and pedals. The car drives itself! Passengers have room to relax as this car of the future drives them down the road.

Testing, Testing...

One of the key components to developing a self-driving car is testing. This often has to be done on a closed track or on public roads when a driver is in the vehicle. It will take many hours of testing before driverless cars are ready for the real road.

BUILDING A SMART CAR

One of the most important roles when it comes to creating a self-driving car is that of the development engineer. This type of automobile engineer ensures that all of a car's **components** work together in harmony. This is especially key when creating a car that has no driver!

The car must be able to predict what is about to happen, make quick changes, and function without running into anything or anyone. Traditional car companies such as Ford and Volkswagen have jumped into the race to create an autonomous car.

But start-ups and tech companies such as Uber and Google have started their own projects at the same time. Why do all of these companies want to create a self-driving car?

This self-driving minivan, designed by Waymo (Google), can take an entire family wherever it needs to go!

Tech Companies Get into the Auto Business

Some people think that a company such as Apple or Waymo will create the best self-driving car. These companies don't have backgrounds in automobiles, but they are innovative and technologically advanced.

Waymo has been developing and testing a new self-driving vehicle, the Firefly 1. The Firefly is a subcompact car.

The engineering behind this type of smart car began with a "What if?" question. What if cars drove themselves?

Self-driving cars could help reduce accidents and give humans more time to be productive instead of sitting in traffic. They could clear up congested roadways, especially in countries such as China and India where there are massive amounts of cars and people.

In cities like Beijing, China and Los Angeles, California, traffic is often congested. Self-driving cars could help speed up traffic, helping people to get where they need to go without the headache of sitting on the road.

Many companies joined together to design, build, and test their own versions of the technology. Someday, manufacturing engineers will ensure the proper production of self-driving cars to be purchased by the public.

DRIVING THROUGH HISTORY

During the 1800s, gasoline engines became the top choice for automobile engineers. Gasoline was cheap and easy to find, and it could power all kinds of vehicles.

Gasoline used to be cheap. Here, it was only 18 cents a gallon! Now it often reaches more than three dollars a gallon.

Now we know that gasoline is a **nonrenewable** resource that pumps harmful gases into our environment. To solve this problem, many engineers have designed their own alternatives to the traditional gasoline engine.

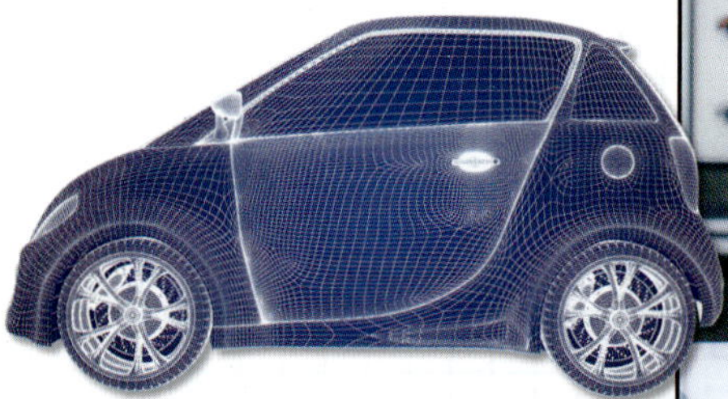

One of the most popular solutions is the use of alternative fuel. Using corn, soybeans, methane, natural gas, hydrogen, or vegetable oil, a specially-designed engine can run relatively cleanly and efficiently. Fuels made from plants are called biofuels.

Biofuels use plants like corn and soybeans to power vehicles.

Some companies are even testing fuels that are made out of algae! There are many options out there, though some are more popular than others. You may have heard of ethanol or E85, which are two well-known biofuels.

Algae occurs in nature, but it can also be grown in a lab. We don't yet know if it can be grown on the large scale that would be needed in order to use it as an automobile fuel.

In addition to plug-in electric cars and those that run on alternative fuels, some smart cars have adopted different systems that run altogether. Fuel cells **convert** chemical energy from hydrogen and oxygen into electricity, which powers the car.

Fuel Cell Car

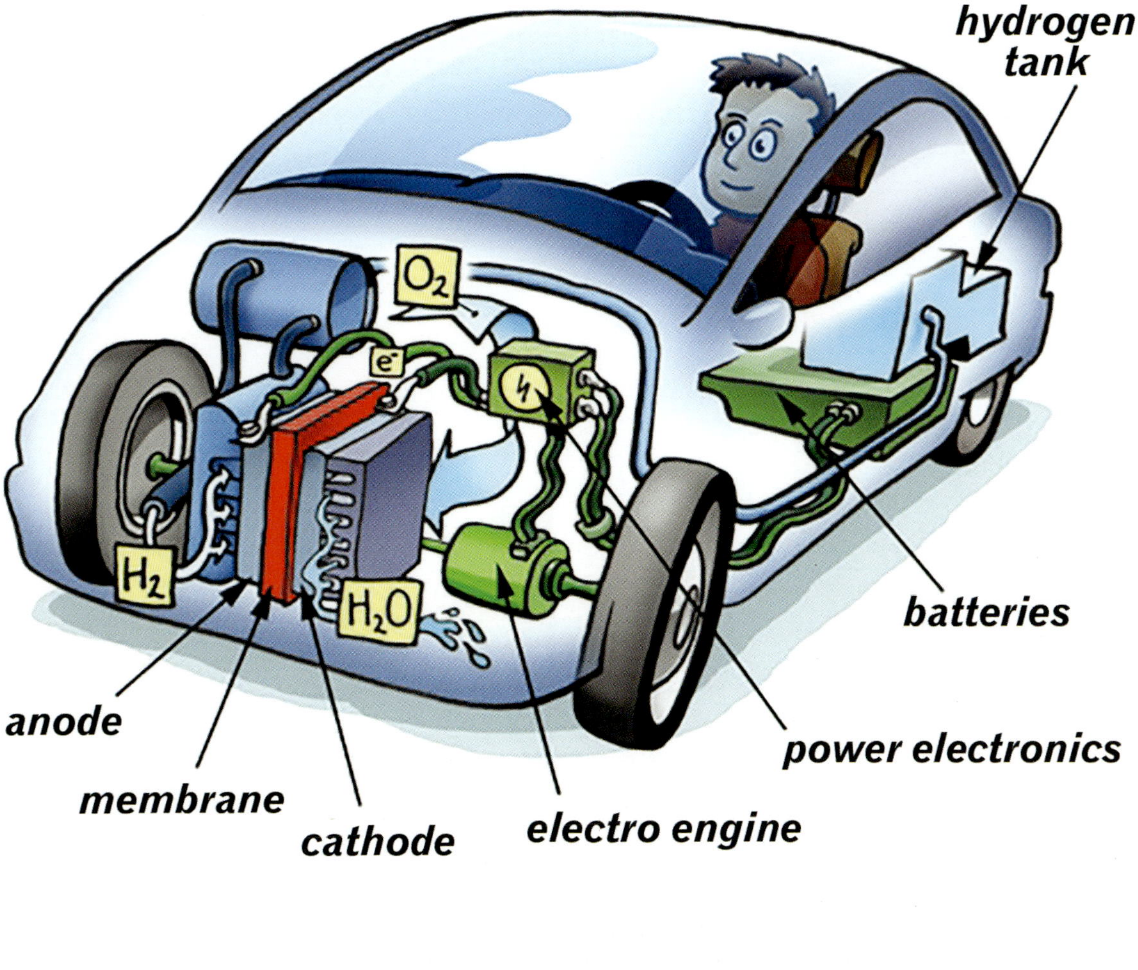

A fuel cell car doesn't have a traditional engine. Instead, it has a variety of components that work together to convert hydrogen and oxygen into energy.

As we move into the future, we can expect to see all kinds of new innovations in auto engineering, especially when it comes to the ways our cars are powered.

Some innovations offer more comfort than safety. The interior of the Mercedes-Benz EQ Silver Arrow includes leather, aluminum, and even wooden features. It also has a touchscreen and a digital cockpit.

When the first automobile engineers built the Model T and other early car designs, they probably didn't imagine all the bells and whistles modern smart cars include. Anti-lock brake systems, backup cameras, seat warmers, and other technologies were all created by **innovative** engineers who dreamed way ahead of their time.

Vehicle backup cameras have become a staple in new cars. They help prevent accidents and make parking a much easier task.

Today, we almost expect these components in our cars and don't bat an eyelash when new features are added, such as in-car Wi-Fi, video players, and high-resolution touchscreens.

Ambient lighting, fragrance systems, and live-streaming TV channels are all details to watch for in the next few years.

The 2020 Mercedes-Benz EQC has futuristic details, like a touchscreen dashboard.

SMART CARS OF THE FUTURE

While fully autonomous cars are still on the horizon, consumers will soon be able to purchase cars that are semi-autonomous, allowing the driver to take his or her hands off the steering wheel and feet off the **accelerator** while the car does most of the driving.

The 2017 Tesla Model X uses Autopilot technology to control the distance between the driver's car and the ones nearby. It also centers the vehicle in the lane.

The autonomous cars of the future will not only solve safety and overcrowding problems, they will make riding in cars a much more enjoyable experience, and allow for seamless deliveries in cars that are driven all by themselves.

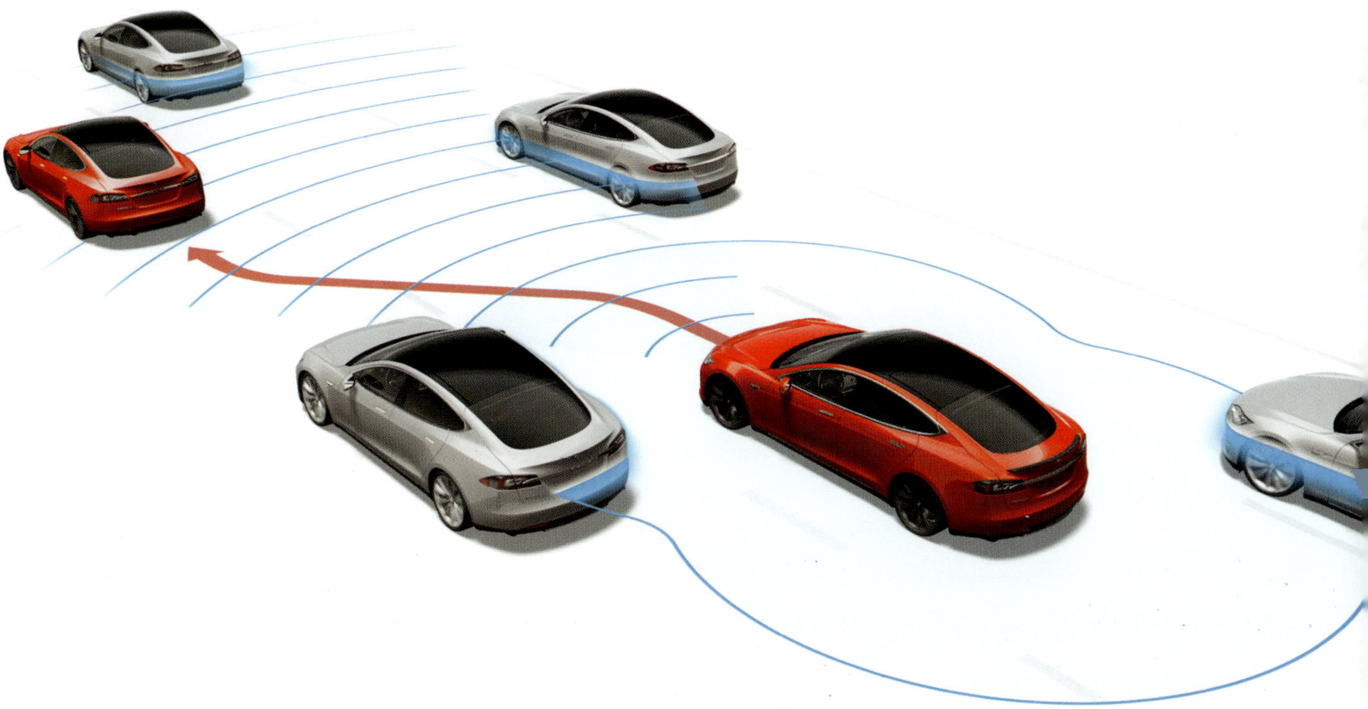

Teslas are already pretty smart! They have Autosteer, Autopark, and other features that offer immense help to the driver.

The automobile engineers of tomorrow have much to be excited about. Self-driving cars, alternative fuels, new body styles, and crazy-cool technologies are all bursting into the industry, and car manufacturers are eager to impress consumers.

The smartest cars of the future will not only be attractive and efficient, but they will need to be environmentally-friendly and full of the latest technology, including autonomous driving options.

Luckily, the smart cars that we will be purchasing in five to ten years are already being designed and engineered. We just have to wait and see what amazing things these innovators are able to produce!

As time goes on, smart cars will become even more sleek and stylish, like their sports car and sedan companions.

TIMELINE

1885 Karl Benz builds the first true automobile. It is powered by a gasoline engine.

1908 Henry Ford's Model T leaves the factory line, cementing gasoline engines as the norm for the next hundred-plus years.

1930 The car radio is introduced.

1939 Air conditioning is added to cars for the first time.

1973 Air bags are introduced, quickly becoming standard.

1992 The Energy Policy Act encourages the development of alternative fuels for cars.

1995 GPS navigation for automobiles is introduced in the United States.

1997 The Toyota Prius goes on sale, becoming the first mass-produced hybrid automobile.

2009 Google begins privately working on self-driving car technology.

2012 A modified Toyota Prius is licensed by the Nevada DMV, becoming the very first licensed driverless car.

2018 The first reported fatal crash involving a driverless car is reported in Arizona.

GLOSSARY

accelerator (ak-SEL-uh-rate-or): a pedal that controls the speed of a motor vehicle

aspects (AS-pekts): features or characteristics of something

atmosphere (AT-muhs-feer): the mixture of gases that surrounds a planet

autonomous (aw-TAH-nuh-muhs): the state of being independent or self-governing

components (kuhm-POH-nuhnts): parts of a larger whole, especially a machine or system

convert (kuhn-VURT): to turn something into something else

debut (day-BYOO): a first public appearance or performance

gasoline (GAS-uh-leen): a liquid fuel made from oil, which is used in many vehicles

hybrid (HYE-brid): something that is made by combining two or more things

innovative (in-uh-VAY-tiv): one way to describe a person who introduces new ideas or inventions

nonrenewable (non-ri-NOO-uh-buhl): sources of power that can be used up

parallel (PAR-uh-lel): staying the same distance from each other and never crossing or meeting

INDEX

SHOW WHAT YOU KNOW

1. What features does a smart car have that set it apart from a traditional car?
2. Why are some engineers designing cars that run on fuels other than gasoline?
3. What innovations in auto technology are helping with safety?
4. How might autonomous cars change the way people live?
5. What are some creative innovations in cars that you would like to see?

FURTHER READING

Diaz, Julio, *Tesla (Vroom! Hot Cars)*, Rourke Educational Media, 2016.

Petersen, Christine, *Inventing the Hybrid Car (Spark of Invention)*, Momentum, 2016.

Vilardi, Debbie, *Electric Cars*, Pop!, 2018.

ABOUT THE AUTHOR

Kaitlyn Duling believes in the power of words to change hearts, minds, and, ultimately, actions. An avid reader and writer who grew up in Illinois, she now lives in Washington, D.C. She knows that knowledge of the past is the key to our future, and wants to ensure that all children and families have access to high-quality information. Kaitlyn has written more than 50 books for children and teens. You can learn more about her at www.kaitlynduling.com.

Meet The Author!
www.meetREMauthors.com

www.rourkeeducationalmedia.com

PHOTO CREDITS: Cover page 1, 3, 14, 22, 23, 44: ©Mercedes-Benz, USA; page 4: ©Rawpixel Ltd.; page 7: ©David Parsons; page 8: ©Vitalij Sova; page 10a, 10b, 35, 45: ©Wiki; page 11a, 32a, 32c: ©gorodenkoff; page 11b: ©da-Kuk; page 12a: ©mattjeacock; page 12b: ©RiverNorthPhotography; page 13: ©Devrimb; page 15: ©Tramino; page 16: ©johnason; page 17: ©400tmax; page 18: ©Honda; page 19: ©Katson80; page 20: ©Lorraine boogich; page 20b: ©JoseGill; page 21, 31: ©LOC; page 24: ©Zapp2Photo; page 26, 27: ©Waymo; page 27: ©WenjieDong; page 30: ©Shinyfamily; page 32b: ©alxpin; page 33: ©Andrew Johnson; page 33: ©feellife; page 34: ©busypix; page 34b: ©tonaquatic; page 26: ©RVT3; page 37: ©Christopher Badzioch; page 41: ©Tesla; page 42: ©metamorworks

Edited by: Keli Sipperley
Cover design by: Rhea Magaro-Wallace
Interior design by: Kathy Walsh

Library of Congress PCN Data

Smart Cars / Kaitlyn Duling
(Engineering Wonders)
ISBN 978-1-64369-027-8 (hard cover)(alk.paper)
ISBN 978-1-64369-112-1 (soft cover)
ISBN 978-1-64369-174-9 (e-Book)
Library of Congress Control Number: 2018956082
Rourke Educational Media
Printed in the United States of America, North Mankato, Minnesota